MY EYES
ARE FOR SEEING

Library of Congress Cataloging-in-Publication Data
Moncure, Jane Belk.
My eyes are for seeing / Jane Belk-Moncure;
illustrated by Viki Woodworth.
p. cm.
Summary: Rhyming text points out that the eyes
can see all things in the world including colors,
shapes, and sizes.
ISBN 1-56766-281-1

1. Vision — Juvenile literature. 2. Eye — Juvenile literature.
[1. Vision. 2. Eye. 3. Senses and sensation.] I. Woodworth,
Viki, ill. II. Title.
QP475.7.M662 1997   97-808
612.8'4 — dc21   CIP
                                                                          AC

BY JANE BELK-MONCURE / ILLUSTRATED BY VIKI WOODWORTH

MY EYES
ARE FOR SEEING

THE CHILD'S WORLD

My eyes see colors all around,
in the air,

on the ground,

4

up above,

down below.
I see colors wherever I go.

My eyes see shapes
when I look up high,
clouds make

pictures in the sky.
Mountains and castles

go floating by. My eyes
help with everything I do.

They help me find the
biggest animals in the zoo,
a giraffe, a polar bear,

an elephant
and a jumpy
kangaroo.

My eyes help me find
tiny animals too:

butterflies and bugs,
an ant and a bee.

I look at them.
They look at me.

Sometimes my eyes
see things up close

like snowflakes
bouncing on my nose

12

or a ladybug
crawling on a rose.

Sometimes I see
things far away
like tiny stars

that fill the skies
or the morning glow
of a bright sunrise.

My eyes are for discovering
baby animals in the spring,

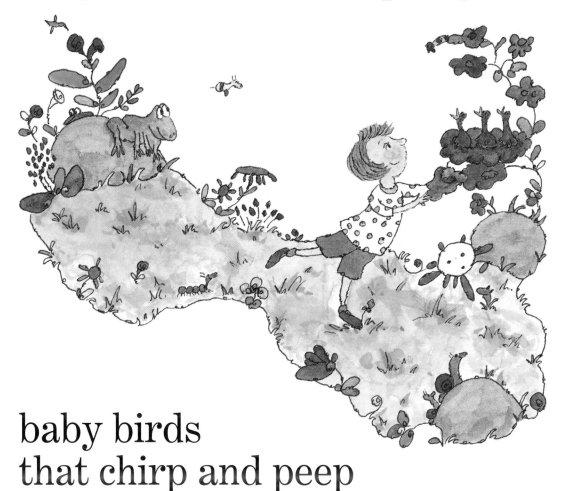

baby birds
that chirp and peep

and a nest of
bunnies fast asleep.

My eyes are with me
everywhere I go,

when I ride my bike,
or take a hike.

My eyes help me explore
places I have never seen before.

They are sunny when I am happy,

rainy when I am sad,

cloudy when I am sleepy and

they sparkle when I am glad.

My eyes are like two windows
I open every day.

They wink, blink and
twinkle as I hop, skip
and play.

My eyes are like a
magic camera,
taking pictures of
my wonderful world.